MVPs

Renardo Barden

The Rourke Corporation, Inc.
Vero Beach, Florida 32964

The Rourke Corporation, Inc.
P.O. Box 3328, Vero Beach, FL 32964

Barden, Renardo.
    MVPs / by Renardo Barden.
        p. cm.— (Baseball heroes)
    Includes index.
    Summary: Traces the origin of the Most Valuable Player award in professional baseball, describes how the players are selected, and highlights the achievements of some of the winners.
    ISBN 0-86593-127-5
        1. Baseball players—United States—Biography—Juvenile literature. [1. Baseball players.]   I Title.   II. Series.
GV865.A1B3238   1991
796.357'092'2—dc20   91-12153
[B]   CIP
                                                                                                      AC

Series Editor: Gregory Lee
Editor: Marguerite Aronowitz
Book design and production: The Creative Spark, Capistrano Beach, CA
Cover photograph: Darrell Sandler/SportsLight
Consultant: Kevin Maingot

Contents

"Mr. October"   5

The First MVP Award   13

Sluggers Versus Pitchers   21

Sportswriters' Choice   29

The Five "Ps" of MVPs   35

Glossary   44

Bibliography   45

Index   47

Reggie Jackson was named MVP only once: in 1973 when he was with the World Series-champion Oakland A's.

"Mr. October"

In 1976 New York Yankee catcher Thurman Munson had 105 runs batted in (RBIs), hit .302, and stole 14 bases. For these skills and his talent with the glove, Munson was named the American League's *Most Valuable Player*, or MVP. He was also a true team leader.

When Munson learned before the 1977 season that Reggie Jackson was joining the team, he was not happy. What could Jackson contribute? After all, the New York team had hot-hitting Mickey Rivers (.312) in the outfield. And to top it off, Munson and his teammates learned that the team's owner had just made Reggie Jackson the highest paid player in baseball.

Also out on the grass for the Yankees was the future manager of the 1990 World Champion Cincinnati Reds, Lou Piniella. Piniella was a good hitter who was getting better. And for home run power, the Yanks already had third baseman Graig Nettles, who had out-homered Jackson 32 to 27 in 1976. Jackson had tremendous power, but he struck out 28 percent of the time—more often than anyone in baseball, and about twice as often as Nettles.

Munson knew Jackson's strengths and weaknesses

Yankee star Don Mattingly was 1984's American League batting champion and the 1985 Most Valuable Player.

as a hitter. After all, he had been behind the plate for the Yankees for seven years and had caught a lot of Jackson's third strikes. Of course he'd also seen a few baseballs fly out of the park in a hurry.

But a case could be made for Jackson's joining the Yankees. For ten years he'd been among the American League (AL) leaders in home runs. He was so strong that it seemed like every time he caught the ball squarely, it left the park. He was also voted AL MVP in 1973 after leading the league in home runs and RBIs. Jackson was a great pressure hitter, perhaps the best ever when a game was on the line. Munson and the rest of the team waited to see what would happen.

Jackson's 1977 season was a stormy one. Shortly after he began playing for the Yankees, Manager Billy Martin benched him in the middle of a televised game— accusing him of loafing in the outfield. When Jackson boasted that the team would be lost without him, bad feelings were created among fans and teammates alike.

Not surprisingly, Jackson was soon unhappy in New York. He told a reporter that he could barely bring himself to go to the ballpark. He ended up with a so-so season, hitting .286 with 32 homers and 110 RBIs. Not bad, but nothing special for a man with Jackson's power. Meanwhile, Graig Nettles hit more homers with a lot less talk. Not to be showed up by Jackson, Munson, Piniella, and Rivers all hit for higher averages.

Jackson continued to hit poorly in the league playoffs against the Kansas City Royals. And he couldn't get going in the first three games of the 1977 World Series against the Los Angeles Dodgers. But in game four, his bat suddenly woke up. First Reggie hit a double off Doug Rau. Then, in his next at-bat, he hit a home run over the left field fence off Rick Rhoden. In Game

Five Reggie slugged another homer—this time off Don Sutton.

By Game Six, the Dodgers had to win just to stay alive. Dodger pitcher Burt Hooten walked Jackson his first time at bat. Then, in the fourth inning, with the Dodgers ahead 3-2, Munson singled. Jackson came up and launched Hooten's first pitch over the right field fence, putting the Yankees ahead 4-3. Unless the Dodgers could reclaim the lead, the Yankees would win the World Series.

In the fifth inning, with Mickey Rivers aboard, Jackson swung for only the third time in two games—another incredible home run. The crowd went wild. Jackson was showing his stuff.

In the eighth inning, Jackson once again stepped into the batter's box. The capacity crowd in Yankee Stadium screamed for another home run. Dodger pitcher Charlie Hough got a knuckleball up. Sure enough, Jackson liked the look of it and bashed it deep into the centerfield stands. Jackson went nuts. So did the Yankee fans. If the World Series had been a boxing match, the referee would have stopped the fight right then.

Now Munson and the rest of the Yankee critics fell silent. Jackson had lived out the daydreams of 50 million would-be major leaguers. He was the World Series hero others only dreamed of being.

It was the perfect way to win a World Series. Although he had hit five home runs in the six-game Series and batted .450, what Jackson would always be remembered for was that with only four swings in two games, he had hit four home runs.

So did Reggie—now "Mr. October"— become the 1977 MVP for this home run binge? No. Although special MVPs for the playoff games and the Series are chosen, the real MVP Awards are given to players based on their regular season play. The 1977 winner was Minnesota second baseman Rod Carew, who managed something almost as extraordinary as Jackson. Carew hit .388 on an otherwise lackluster team.

Jackson And Schmidt: Birds Of A Feather

Although they spent their entire careers in different leagues, Reggie Jackson and Philadelphia Phillies MVP third baseman Mike Schmidt have many things in common. They played at the same time in baseball history, and are currently ranked seventh and sixth among the top home run hitters of all time. Each hit more round trippers than Ted Williams, Lou Gehrig, or Mickey Mantle.

Jackson might have won more home run titles if he didn't have to compete against some of the greatest American League home run hitters ever, including Harmon Killebrew (AL MVP 1969) and Carl Yastrzemski (AL MVP 1967). Schmidt also had tough competition: Willie Stargell (NL MVP 1979), George Foster, Dave Kingman, Dale Murphy (NL MVP 1982, 1983), and Johnny Bench (NL MVP 1970, 1972).

Although Jackson played longer than Schmidt and had about 1,000 more at-bats, their statistics are much alike. Schmidt's lifetime average of about .269 compares with Jackson's .262. Schmidt's on-base percentage and slugging averages are slightly higher than Jackson's, partly because Reggie struck out so often. But Schmidt was no stranger to the strikeout, either.

Jackson never won another MVP honor after 1973. Schmidt won the National League (NL) MVP award in 1980, 1981 and 1986. Before Schmidt, only Joe

9

Phillies third baseman Mike Schmidt took MVP honors three times in the 1980s—a remarkable achievement.

DiMaggio, Stan Musial, Mickey Mantle, Roy Campanella and Yogi Berra had won three times.

Once they took off their batting helmets, Schmidt and Jackson were very different players. Schmidt was a great fielder, a winner of eight Gold Glove Awards at third base, and a devoted team player. Jackson was not a good defensive player, and seemed to think of himself as a one-man team.

So why did Mike Schmidt win three MVP Awards compared with Jackson's one? It's tempting to say that Schmidt's great fielding and throwing made the difference, but fielding has never carried much weight with MVP voters. It's more likely that Schmidt won his awards based on popularity. Most baseball writers and fans found it easier to like the modest, plain-spoken Schmidt than the self-promoting Jackson.

The one thing Jackson seems to have done better than Schmidt—or anybody—was to get important hits under conditions of extreme pressure. Schmidt was in fewer World Championship games and had fewer chances to hit under pressure.

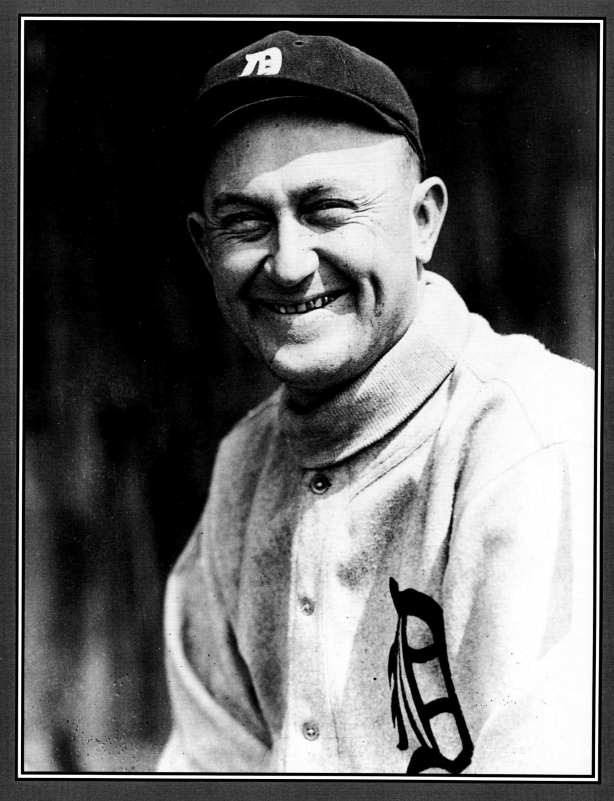

*Ty Cobb, one of the greatest hitters of all time, was the first player
to be recognized as "most valuable player."*

The First MVP Award

Just before the beginning of the 1910 baseball season, car company owner Hugh Chalmers had a bright idea. An avid baseball fan, he decided to give away one of his new Chalmers "30" automobiles to the major league batter having the highest batting average in the upcoming season. Chalmers' rules were simple. A regular player had to have at least 350 at bats, but catchers and pitchers could qualify with fewer.

Sounds a lot like today's giveaways, right? Sure. Chalmers was the forerunner of the tire, athletic shoes, razor blades, beer, and insurance companies that advertise with

---

MVP Trivia

Q: Name the only pitcher to ever win the MVP by unanimous vote.
A: Carl Hubbell, in 1936.

Q: What great MVP pitcher was described as being able to "throw a lamb chop past a wolf?"
A: Sportswriter Bugs Baer wrote those lines about 1931 MVP Lefty Grove of the Philadelphia Athletics.

Q: A Phillies pitcher once said "trying to sneak a fastball by him is like trying to sneak the sunrise past a rooster." Name the hitter he was describing.
A: Hank Aaron.

Q: This NL pitcher and four-time Cy Young Award winner never received an MVP award. Who was he?
A: Steve Carlton.

Willie McGee, named MVP in 1985, was still showing his stuff when he won the National League batting title in 1990.

sports-oriented gimmicks. Chalmers realized that for the price of his cheapest model, he could get the name of his car before millions of baseball fans.

Baseball greats like Don Mattingly, Jose Canseco and Kirk Gibson—all hot batting MVPs—may not get very excited about winning a new car today. After all, they earn the equivalent of a new car for every game they play. But in 1910, even the best ballplayers were lucky to earn the price of a new car (in 1910 dollars) in an entire year. To them, a new car was a real bonus.

If George Brett had been around in 1910, he might have won the Chalmers. In 1980 he won the American

League MVP by batting .390. Rod Carew won the AL MVP in 1977 for batting .388. Brett and Carew are the only two hitters to hit better than .380 since Ted Williams hit .388 in 1957. But in 1910, a .380 average wouldn't have cut it. The Chalmers would go to one of two American League players: Ty Cobb or Napolean "Nap" Lajoie.

Ty Cobb: The Dead Ball Demon

When former baseball player and manager Leo Durocher said "Nice guys finish last," he was probably thinking of a ruthless Detroit outfielder named Ty Cobb. Cobb was not a nice guy, and he was never known to have finished last at anything.

When it comes to batting records, only a couple of other baseball players in the history of the game compare to Cobb. His lifetime batting average is the highest ever recorded: .366. He's second in hits, third in stolen bases, fourth in total bases, fifth in runs batted in, and first in runs produced. Cobb hit over .300 for 23 years in a row, led the league a dozen times, and hit .400 or better three times.

Cobb spent much of his career during the *dead ball* era, when baseballs were made differently. The dead ball did not carry the way modern cork-centered baseballs do. It seemed pointless trying to hit it out. To get some hits against the dead ball, Cobb used a hands-apart grip on the bat, was an excellent bunter, and "poked" hits through gaps in the infield.

Great as he was, Cobb was disliked by many. When things didn't go his way, he used his fists and cleats on teammates, umpires, managers, opposing players, hotel managers and fans alike. To protect himself from his enemies, he slept with a pistol under

Kirk Gibson's 1988 MVP season with the Los Angeles Dodgers reached a rousing finale when he homered to win Game One of the World Series against the Oakland A's.

his pillow—particularly when traveling on trains with his teammates.

Even 20 or 30 years after his last time at bat, many of Cobb's fellow ballplayers refused to speak to him at "old timer's" games. When he died in 1961, only three men in baseball came to his funeral.

Back in 1910, however, Cobb had captured the American League batting title for three years in a row. He also made himself a terror on the basepaths—stealing 76 bases in 1909. He was the leading contender for the Chalmers.

The Seven Bunts of Nap Lajoie

A few years older and more popular than Cobb, Nap Lajoie was the quiet, graceful second baseman for the Cleveland Bronchos. He was the league's star hitter before Cobb.

In 1910, writers accused Cobb of pursuing the Chalmers at the expense of helping the Tigers win the pennant. Nobody said the same of Lajoie. In fact, for nearly half a century, Lajoie's 1901 batting average had been wrongly computed to be .405 rather than the .422 it actually was! It's hard to imagine that a player today would be so unconcerned about his own batting average that he wouldn't notice the error.

The final day of the big Chalmers' contest was October 9, 1910. Cobb decided to stand pat at .383 and sat the game out. Lajoie had a .376 average and looked like a certain second place. But it wasn't over yet. The Cleveland team was slated for a double header against the St. Louis Browns.

The Browns were managed by Jack O'Connor, a man who intensely disliked Cobb. He instructed his rookie third baseman, Red Corriden, to play way back

*The ever-dependable Stan Musial of the St. Louis Cardinals won
the MVP award three times in the 1940s.*

from third base whenever Lajoie came up to bat.

Lajoie went eight for eight that day, including seven bunts down the third baseline. For Lajoie, whose days as a base stealer were behind him, this was remarkable. But because Corriden was deep, he couldn't get to the ball in time to throw Lajoie out. None of Lajoie's seven bunts were ruled errors. So when the averages were tallied up, Lajoie had slipped past Cobb.

Many felt sure that O'Connor had been trying to "get" Cobb and deprive him of the batting title. As a result, O'Connor lost his job as manager.

Today, Lajoie is listed as the winner of the 1910 batting title. Since feelings had run strong for both Cobb and Lajoie, the car manufacturer took the easy way out. He gave each player a Chalmers automobile.

Kevin Mitchell's fence-busting '89 season continued the tendency to reward power hitters with MVP honors.

Sluggers Versus Pitchers

Chalmers was determined not to repeat the mistakes of 1910. One thing was sure. He would not again use the "science" of batting averages to determine the winner. Instead, he decided to give a car to one player in the National League and one player in the American League. The cars would go to "the most important and useful player to his club."

Decisions were to be made by a committee: one baseball writer from each major league city was to vote for eight players. A first place vote was worth eight points, a second place, seven, and so on. The cars were to be given to the players with the highest number of points.

When the votes were in, Cobb's .402 batting average and 83 stolen bases could not be overlooked by American League voters, even though Cobb continued to be unpopular. He received all the available first place votes, and drove away in another Chalmers.

Coming up to modern times, 48 major league players in 1990 hit 21 home runs or more. But in 1911 when Chicago Cubs outfielder Frank Schulte hit 21, only two other players had ever hit more. Schulte's lucky 21 was seen as an eye-popping feat, and won him the NL MVP. In many ways Schulte's award set the stage for the age of home runs. The new, cork-centered baseball introduced in the major leagues the year before changed the game for good.

Back-to-back MVP honors? Dale Murphy (above) accomplished that feat in 1982-83 with the Atlanta Braves, and Roger Maris (right) did the same with the 1960-61 Yankees.

The Schulte award of 1911 began the trend of using home run power and batting statistics at the expense of fielding and pitching in determing greatness. It was the first—but not the last time—that the MVP Award went to a hot home run hitter instead of a deserving pitcher.

Hitters continued to win the Chalmers Award until 1913, when Washington pitcher Walter Johnson won with an awesome 36 wins, an ERA of 1.14, and 243 strikeouts. This was an accomplishment that even home run-crazed MVP voters couldn't ignore.

After five years, Chalmers stopped giving the award. The major leagues could have kept it alive, but they were concerned with business competition from a third baseball league, the Federal League. Then came

Sandy Koufax was unbeatable in 1963, winning the argument between sluggers and pitchers in the MVP voting.

World War I, and the country's attention turned to Europe. The Federal League did not last and the war was over shortly after America became involved in it.

The American and National Leagues did not immediately restore awards for individual players because Ty Cobb and other players sought to use their Chalmers Awards to negotiate better salaries for themselves. The league owners resented this, even though in those days, ballplayers were poorly paid. The owners did not think they should be paid a lot of money. Ballplayers were hard enough to handle when they were poor.

Money Or Sportsmanship?

Shortly after World War I, baseball was hurt by a series of scandals involving gamblers, money, and the throwing of games by baseball players. Some of the greatest players of the day were involved and banned from baseball. Many other players were thought to be involved in gambling and game fixing.

Partly to win back public support, the major leagues decided to bring back the Most Valuable Player awards. In 1922 the American League Trophy Committee was formed—but not to give away expensive new cars. Trophies were what the owners had in mind.

The American League rules called for eight baseball writers (one from each American League city) to select the most valuable player from each team and rank them one through eight. But the new system created problems. Players who also served as managers were ineligible, which meant several top players would be left off the ballot. And since only one player could be named from each team, many outstanding players often got no votes at all. For example, George Sisler, the great

Baseball manager and Hall of Famer Frank Robinson is the only player to have won MVP honors in both major leagues.

St. Louis Browns first baseman, won the first award in 1922. He was named on all eight ballots, which meant none of the writers could cast a single vote for his worthy teammate Ken Williams, who had hit 39 home runs that year.

Worst of all, the rules said that no one player could be his team's—or the league's—MVP more than once. So, for example, in 1927 Babe Ruth could not be considered for the award despite his record 60 home runs (he had won the award in 1923). Lou Gehrig won in 1927, and after that neither Ruth nor Gehrig could win again. They were the number one and two home run hitters for the next five years in a row.

The National League created a much better system. It allowed writers to vote for 10 NL players rather than eight. Voters were allowed to vote for any player, even those on the same team. And best of all, previous winners were eligible.

But by the end of 1929, both leagues did away with the MVP awards because once again, players were attempting to use their awards to negotiate higher salaries from team owners.

Lucky for the players, however, the awards had caught on with the public. Fans found them useful in helping them keep track of the players' achievements.

Jose Canseco's 1988 MVP award capped a year when he started the "40-40 Club," stealing more than 40 bases and hitting 42 homers.

Sportswriters' Choice

In 1929 the Baseball Writers Association of America (BBWAA) announced the results of their AL MVP award. They named Lou Fonseca, a Cleveland first baseman who had hit .369 for the Tribe. Two months later, writers from a rival publication called the *Sporting News* declared that the true "unofficial" AL MVP was Al Simmons, a Philadelphia outfielder who hit .365 with 34 home runs that year. Today, although the *Sporting News* continues to give out its annual awards, the accepted MVP Awards are those given by the BBWAA.

In 1930 the BBWAA decided to appoint two committees of writers (one per league) to elect

---

MVP Trivia

Q: Who is the only catcher to be named Rookie of the Year, MVP, receive a Gold Glove and be elected to the Hall of Fame?
A: Thurman Munson.

Q: Where will you find the names of more catchers—in the Hall of Fame, or on the list of MVPs?
A: More catchers have been elected to the Hall of Fame than have been voted MVPs.

Q: Who are the only two players to have hit more than 500 home runs but never be named MVPs?
A: Eddie Mathews (512) and Mel Ott (511).

Q: Who was the last player unanimously voted MVP?
A: Oakland's Jose Canseco, in 1988.

MVPs and "to award suitable emblems to the players selected." Their modern approach to MVP selection eliminated most of the obvious flaws of earlier methods.

Today 52 BBWAA writers (two for each team in both leagues) participate in the selection process. Each voter selects ten players and ranks them one through ten in order of value of the players' contributions. Each voter then returns the ballot before any League Championship Series games begin, so that voting is not affected by what players do in the playoff games or World Series. Before voting, each writer receives a copy of the MVP selection guidelines. These guidelines ask the voter to consider the following:

1. The actual value of the player to his team—strength of both offense and defense.

2. The number of games played.

3. General character, disposition, loyalty and effort.

Each year an amendment is added to the ballot that reads, "All players are eligible, including pitchers, both starters and relievers." The view that pitchers cannot or should not be given fair consideration as MVPs, however, seems to persist.

Should Pitchers Be MVPs?

Should a player who participates only in every fourth or fifth game be considered as valuable as one who plays every day?

Some fans say that since a pitcher does not play every day, he makes a limited contribution to his team. They also remind us that in the American League a pitcher does not even have to hit. And they point out that a starting pitcher may pitch for only four or five innings every fifth day. At this pace, a starter may only appear for nine innings once every two weeks. Relief pitchers come into the game more often, but most stay for fewer innings than starting pitchers. Playing time, say these same fans, is an important factor.

Former California Angels third baseman Doug DeCinces says that, in his opinion, "relievers can be MVPs, because they're in half the games. But, starters who go out every fourth or fifth day—no way."

Others argue that pitchers handle the ball on every play— more than any other player except the catcher. They also say that the pitcher determines how well the other team will hit, and that no other player on the field has so much power to affect the opposing team. This, they argue, is a big contribution.

Yet Kansas City Royals first baseman George Brett feels strongly that pitchers should not be given MVPs. "I don't think it should be a pitcher. That's why they have a Cy Young Award, so the guys who sit around in the bullpen and the dugout and do crossword puzzles and eat nachos and come up to the clubhouse and practice their putting strokes and get in attendance pools every night—so those guys can have their own award."

Cincinnati Reds manager Lou Piniella is a bit more inclined to take the pitcher's side. "I might not have seen it that way as a player, but believe me, if you have a great pitcher to throw out there every day, it's invaluable."

Boston Red Sox veteran Jim Rice takes a broader view. The powerful slugger who knocked 46 home runs and got 213 hits to capture the 1978 AL MVP argues that "the player with the best stats should win."

Counting both leagues, there have been about 150 MVP awards to date. If we divide this number by the

Shortstop Cal Ripken, Jr., has lived up to his '83 MVP recognition with a consistent batting average, the highest fielding percentage (.996) for his position, and a streak of errorless games.

number of field positions (nine), 17 awards would fairly represent each position. To date, there have been more than 20 MVP Awards presented to pitchers. So, in terms of numbers, pitchers are already fairly represented. If a single position has been slighted, it is probably that of catcher. And the catcher handles the ball more often than any other player except the pitcher.

When catchers Yogi Berra and Roy Campanella were behind the plate for the Yankees and Dodgers in the early 1950s, sportswriters voted them MVPs again and again. Between 1951 and 1955, the pair were named MVPs three times each. And Johnny Bench was honored as MVP twice in 1970 and 1972—both years in which he led the league in home runs. But take away these three backstops (all of whom were sluggers) and Mickey Cochrane, Gabby Hartnett, Ernie Lombardi, Elston Howard, and the late Thurman Munson remain. In other words, only eight different catchers have been MVPs on 14 occasions. To qualify, they had to produce an average of 26 homers per season and a combined overall batting average of .305.

Whatever their chances of winning an MVP, pitchers are the only players in baseball who can qualify without being at least partly judged by their bats. In fact, the "no-pitchers-as-MVPs-argument" probably hides the frustration felt by those who are unhappy with the fact that power hitting statistics are what most MVPs have in common. Since 1931, when voting regulations became standardized, most power hitters with the ability to stay consistent have been awarded MVP honors at least once.

A few great hitters like Duke Snider, Eddie Mathews and Al Kaline were never honored as MVPs because it was their misfortune to shine brightest during seasons when other great hitters were outslugging them. Big bats like Ted Williams, Mickey Mantle, Willie Mays, Hank Aaron, Roger Maris, Roy Campanella, Yogi Berra and Harmon Killebrew all took home MVP Awards.

It's interesting that eight of the all time strikeout leaders—Jackson, Stargell, Schmidt, Mantle, Killebrew, McCovey, Frank Robinson and Willie Mays—were named MVPs at least once.

Robin Yount, two-time MVP winner, is an example of the player who labors hard with an also-ran team, such as the Milwaukee Brewers.

The Five "Ps" Of MVPs

T he MVP contest most often comes down to what might be called the five "Ps": Power, Personality, Popularity, Place and Position.

Power

Most of the best home run hitters have been named MVPs at least once. Some—like Gehrig, DiMaggio and Williams—have hit for high batting averages as well. But home runs and RBIs have proven to be more important than mere batting averages. "Power" can also describe pitchers. MVP-winning pitchers have tended to be flamethrowers like Boston's Roger Clemens who won the award in 1986; Cardinal Bob Gibson who won in 1968; Philadelphia's Lefty Grove who won in 1931; or Washington's Walter Johnson, who won in 1913.

Personality

Hank Aaron, the all-time home run hitter and all-time RBI leader, had an amazing career with the bat. He led the league in homers four times, RBIs four times, doubles four times, average twice, hits twice, and runs scored three times. Yet only once did he win the MVP—in 1957—when his team, the Milwaukee Braves, won the World Series. What was "Hammerin' Hank's" feat that year? He hit .322, scored 118 runs, spanked a league-leading 44 home runs, and drove in 132 RBIs.

Toward the end of his career, Aaron complained that he didn't get his fair share of recognition. But this was partly because he had to compete for publicity with Willie Mays, Ted Williams, Ernie Banks, Mickey Mantle, Roy Campanella, Yogi Berra, and even Reggie Jackson. Campanella, Mantle and Berra were all three-time MVPs; while Mays, Williams and Banks were each two-time winners. Aaron was right, however, about the neglect. He was quiet and reserved, and behaved according to what was expected of him. He just didn't have the outgoing personality of a Mays or a Berra.

Popularity

Ted Williams, "the Splendid Splinter," had personality but not popularity. One of the greatest hitters of all time, Williams was often moody and less than charming. His feuds with sportswriters and fans were the stuff of legend. A two-time MVP winner, Williams was so dominant that he might have won more often if he had been more popular.

In 1947 this great Red Sox outfielder won the *Triple Crown*: He had the highest batting average (.343), the most home runs (32) and the most runs batted in (114). But the sportswriters chose instead the charming Yankee Clipper, Joe DiMaggio, as MVP. Of course, DiMaggio was a great player, yet in '47 he was eclipsed by Williams. "Joltin' Joe" had hit .315 with 20 home runs, and 97 runs batted in, while Williams had him beat in every department except smiles for the camera.

Place

Television audiences have made the game a little more fair for players in cities such as Milwaukee,

Harmon Killebrew only won the MVP once (1969) playing for the underdog Minnesota Twins. But he finally got his due when he was elected to the Hall of Fame. Killebrew is fifth on the all-time home run list (573).

Minneapolis, Seattle, Houston, Cleveland and Atlanta. But not that much.

The East and West Coasts are rich in baseball traditions. Big established teams like the Yankees, Dodgers, Red Sox and Giants have always drawn top players and paid the salaries needed to keep them. Newer teams with smaller crowds and less money, however, have often been forced to try to build winning teams around a single star player.

Aaron spent his entire career with the Braves ballclub, first in Milwaukee and then in Atlanta. In these cities he played before smaller crowds and on teams that were rarely in the pennant race. It's clear that Aaron suffered from poor exposure, and would have fared much better in the era of cable television.

Another powerful slugger who suffered from an even worse case of neglect was Harmon Killebrew, the right-handed first baseman who started out so quietly with the Washington Senators. A contemporary of Aaron's, Killebrew began playing full time for the Senators in 1959. Amazingly, he went from 0 home runs in 1958 to 42 in 1959.

But during the next few years, nobody seemed to notice him or take him seriously. American League fans were still caught up in the sensational careers of MVPs like Williams, Mantle and Maris. Mantle and Maris were everybody's darlings, especially after their dual fence-busting season of 1961. Meanwhile, back in Minnesota (after the Senators became the Twins), Killebrew quietly blew all of them out of the water. He slammed 476 home runs between 1959 and 1970, for an average of just under 40 per year for 12 years. But he had to work his way up to MVP status one notch at a time. Killebrew received just 21 votes in 1959, but by

1969 he earned 264 and won. That year, "the Killer" crashed 49 home runs, chalked up 144 RBIs, and drew 145 bases on balls.

Killebrew was that rare creature among sluggers, a batter who rarely struck out. Reggie Jackson, who banged 47 homers of his own the year Killebrew hit 49, could have taken lessons in patience from Killebrew. Only one American League baseball player has ever hit more home runs—the 1923 AL MVP, Babe Ruth, "The Sultan of Swat."

Somebody else who needed lessons in patience was Killebrew's frisky teammate, Rod Carew. As it happened, the year Killebrew finally got his due from MVP voters was also a big year for Rod Carew. In 1969 Carew led the American League in hitting with .332 and, more dramatically, he stole home nine times during the season.

Carew, who joined the Minnesota Twins as a 21-year-old second baseman in 1967, won the American League batting title seven times (1969, 1972, 1973, 1974, 1975, 1977 and 1978). He has recently been inducted into the Hall of Fame. Only Honus Wagner and Ty Cobb won more batting championships than Carew.

Current star Wade Boggs has a higher lifetime batting average than Carew's .328, but Boggs has been overlooked for the MVP Award partly due to his lack of power.

Like Boggs, Carew never hit with power. Unlike Boggs, Carew was a speedster on the basepaths. He stole home 16 times in his career, more than any other player except for Jackie Robinson and Frankie Frisch. But much of his base stealing and singles-hitting went unrecognized.

Like Killebrew, Carew had to work his way up the

Rod Carew hit his 3,000th hit while playing for the California Angels. The seven-time AL batting champion was MVP in his hottest year—1977.

MVP list. He won 30 votes in 1969, 16 votes in 1972, 83 votes in 1973, 70 in 1974, 54 in 1975 and 71 in 1976, before finally winning the honor with 273 in 1977. That year Carew hit a remarkable .388, fully 52 percentage points ahead of the second place hitter!

Position

Some people complain about the shortage of catchers and shortstops among MVP winners. But the winning position isn't so much where a player stands on the field, but rather where his team finishes in the standings.

Veteran manager Sparky Anderson said that he

thinks MVPs should be chosen because of what they contribute to their teams. He even says that MVPs should come from winning teams. George Brett agrees, adding that an MVP should be a player who could not be removed from the lineup without sinking the team's chances to stay in the pennant race. Generally speaking, MVP voters agree with these views. About 70 percent of MVP winners have been selected from either first place or pennant-winning teams.

Big exceptions have been 1989 MVP Robin Yount, and the 1977 award that went to Rod Carew when he hit .388.

The MVP On Defense

Where among all these MVPs, ask some fans, are the great defensive players, the fielders? It's true that Johnny Bench and Mike Schmidt were MVPs, but Schmidt and Bench were sluggers who could not be ignored. Likewise it was easy to pick 1984 NL MVP Ryne Sandberg, Cubs second baseman, who got the award for hitting .314 and scoring 114 runs. So where among the NL MVPs is Ozzie Smith, one of the premier base stealers of all time and perhaps the greatest shortstop ever to put on a glove? Brooks Robinson, the incomparable Baltimore Orioles third baseman, made it in 1964. But that was the year he hit for his all-time high of .317. Johnny Bench, a ten-year Gold Glove catcher for the Cincinnati Reds, was named MVP twice in years when he had hit 40 home runs or more.

Don't look for Gold Gloves among the MVPs. If Gold Glove winners are among the MVPs, it's probably because of the heft of their bats rather than the accuracy of their throwing arms.

The brainchild of the Rawlings Sporting Goods

Everyone loves a hitter, and the 1987 MVP season of George Bell saw him hit .308, including 47 homers.

Company, the Gold Glove Awards were first given in 1957. But they, too, have been influenced by the offensive abilities of players. Today, major league players themselves vote for Gold Glove winners, but players with the highest fielding averages are often bypassed by players with flashy styles and hot bats.

How To Pick The MVPs Of The Future

In trying to pick future MVPs, first remember the Five "Ps." Then look at those with a shot at joining the exclusive "500 Club": hitters with 500 or more career homers.

Who are the big power hitters of today who might join Schmidt and Jackson in "The 500 Club"?

Long-time powerhouse Dave Winfield is close, but he's getting up there in years and is troubled by bad knees. Dale Murphy, Eddie Murray and Andre Dawson aren't getting any younger, but they're great power hitters with an outside chance to crack 500. Darryl Strawberry has a good chance if he keeps his home run stroke hot in Los Angeles. But like all 500 lifetime home run hitters, he'll have to start racking up some 40-plus seasons.

First baseman Fred McGriff has a long way to go, as does another outstanding first baseman—Mark McGwire. Yet each of them seems to have turned 30 homers a year into a routine. Jose Canseco has the stroke, of course, but players with such muscular upper bodies are prone to the sorts of neck and back problems that Canseco has already experienced. Cecil Fielder has shown a flash of great power, but he's a little late getting started if he wants to chase the home run leaders. And he'll have to keep his weight down or pitchers will learn to take advantage of him.

The home run hitters of today and tomorrow are typically the MVPs of tomorrow. But with pitchers like Roger Clemens, Dwight Gooden, and others pulling down big dollars, look for media attention to shift a little away from sluggers standing at the plate to players scuffing the pitching rubber. As salaries grow, the danger is that baseball players and fans alike will pay more attention to numbers, statistics and salaries than to team contributions. If that happens, the name "most valuable player" will take on a completely different meaning.

Glossary

BATTING AVERAGE. A statistic figured by dividing the number of hits a batter gets by the number of times he's at bat.

DEAD BALL. In the early days of the game, the baseball was larger, heavier, and didn't carry as far.

GRAND SLAM. A home run with the bases loaded.

LIVE BALL. Today's baseball is lighter, with a cork center, that travels farther when hit.

MOST VALUABLE PLAYER (MVP). The annual award given to one player from each league by the Baseball Writers Association of America. MVP candidates are judged by their entire season's contribution to their team in both offensive and defensive categories.

RBIs. Runs batted in. The number of base runners the batter manages to score during his time at bat.

SLUGGING PERCENTAGE. A statistic figured by dividing the total number of bases a batter gets by the number of times he's at bat.

TRIPLE CROWN. When a player ends the season leading the league in home runs, batting average, and RBIs.

Bibliography

Allen, Lee. *The National League Story*. New York: Hill & Wang, 1965.

Asinof, Eliot. *Eight Men Out.* New York: Henry Holt, 1987.

Ercolano, Patrick. *Fungoes, Floaters, and Fork Balls: A Colorful Baseball Dictionary.* Englewood Cliffs, New Jersey: Prentice-Hall, 1987.

Dewan, John, Don Zminda and Stats, Inc. *The Stats Baseball Scoreboard.* New York: Ballantine Books, 1990.

Honig, Donald. *The Greatest First Basemen of All Time.* New York: Crown Publishers, 1988.

—-. *The Greatest Pitchers of All Time.* New York: Crown Publishers, 1988.

Reichler, Joseph. *Baseball's Great Moments.* New York: Bonanza Books, 1986.

Ritter, Lawrence and Donald Honig. *The 100 Greatest Baseball Players of All Time.* New York: Crown Publishers, 1986.

Hernandez, Keith and Mike Bryan. *If At First...A Season with the Mets.* New York: McGraw-Hill, 1986.

Thorn, John and Pete Palmer, eds. *Total Baseball*. New York: Warner Books, 1989.

Neft, David S. and Richard M. Cohen. *The Sports Encyclopedia: Baseball*. New York: St. Martin's Press, 1987.

Index

Aaron, Hank, 13, 33, 35-36, 38

Banks, Ernie, 36
Bench, Johnny, 9, 32-33, 41
Berra, Yogi, 11, 32, 33, 36
Boggs, Wade, 39
Brett, George, 14-15, 31, 41

Campanella, Roy, 11, 32, 33, 36
Canseco, Jose, 14, 29, 43
Carew, Rod, 9, 15, 39-40, 41
Carlton, Steve, 13
Clemens, Roger, 35, 43
Cobb, Ty, 15-19, 21, 25, 39

Dawson, Andre, 43
dead ball, 15
DeCinces, Doug, 31
DiMaggio, Joe, 11, 35, 36

Fielder, Cecil, 43
Fonseca, Lou, 29

Gehrig, Lou, 9, 27, 35
Gibson, Bob, 35
Gibson, Kirk, 14
Gold Glove Awards, 11, 41-42
Grove, Lefty, 13, 35

Hubbell, Carl, 13

Jackson, Reggie, 5-11, 33, 36, 39, 43
Johnson, Walter, 23, 35

Kaline, Al, 33
Killebrew, Harmon, 9, 33, 38-39

Lajoie, Napolean ("Nap"), 15, 17-19

Mantle, Mickey, 9, 11, 33, 36, 38
Maris, Roger, 33, 38
Mathews, Eddie, 29, 33
Mattingly, Don, 14
Mays, Willie, 33, 36
McGriff, Fred, 43

McGwire, Mark, 43
Most Valuable Player (MVP) Award,
    and catchers, 32-33
    and the five "Ps," 35-42
    and pitchers, 30-32
    defined, 30
    the AL Trophy Committee, 25-27
    the BBWAA Award, 29-30
    the Chalmers Award, 13-15, 17-
        19, 21-25
    the Sporting News Award, 29
Munson, Thurman, 5, 7, 8, 29, 33
Murphy, Dale, 9, 43
Murray, Eddie, 43
Musial, Stan, 11

Nettles, Graig, 5, 7

Ott, Mel, 29

Piniella, Lou, 5, 7, 31

Rice, Jim, 31
Rivers, Mickey, 5, 7, 8
Robinson, Brooks, 41
Robinson, Frank, 33
Ruth, Babe, 27, 39

Sandberg, Ryne, 41
Schmidt, Mike, 9-11, 33, 41, 43
Schulte, Frank, 21
Simmons, Al, 29
Sisler, George, 25-27
Smith, Ozzie, 41
Snider, Duke, 33
Stargell, Willie, 9, 33
Strawberry, Darryl, 43

Williams, Ted, 9, 15, 33, 35, 36, 38
Winfield, Dave, 43

Yastrzemski, Carl, 9
Yount, Robin, 41

About The Author

Renardo Barden is the author of several books, including these titles in the Rourke TROUBLED SOCIETY library: *Cults, Gangs, Gun Control*, and *Prisons*. He is a former sports magazine editor, and currently freelances in New York City.

Photo Credits